"As someone who has devoted the last 28+ years of his life to helping churches accelerate generosity, I am always delighted when I see a good book on the topic. Especially when it is a senior pastor talking about his family's giving! Bruce has written transparently and authentically about the giving journey he and his wife have been on. Not only does he illuminate the biblical references to giving, but he also provides inspiration from his own real life examples. A really fine resource for pastors, church leaders and lay people!"

Jim Sheppard
CEO & Principal, Generis

"For many of us, generosity is more of a begrudging response to fundraising than a joyful response to God. Bruce Miller has written a helpful guide that helps correct that, revealing the wide chasm between the biblical concept of joyful generosity and our modern-day pattern of guilt-driven fundraising. Coupled with its helpful study guides, this book will enable you to think and respond more biblically to the important role that generosity is supposed to play in our walk with Jesus."

Larry Osborne
Pastor & Author, North Coast Church, Vista, California

"This book made me smile. It unlocks the secret of a joyous life through generosity. The lessons here, if applied to your life, will make you smile. And, as Bruce puts it, I think will make God smile as well."

Dave Travis
Strategic Counsel to Pastors & Church Boards, Generis

"In Bruce Miller's new book, *Giving: The Three Questions*, I found each question, the biblical support for the responses to the questions and the recommended action steps to take to be excellent in their simplicity, potent in their content and life transforming as Christians choose to live them out and practically apply them in their daily lives. This book will <u>definitely</u> be a resource for me and one that will be referred to regularly on this critical, biblical topic. I **highly recommend** this book for every believer in Jesus Christ who desires to grow in spiritual maturity and the joy that giving brings!"

Bart Salmon, Assistant Vice President for Facilities
Rice University
Advisor (Elder), Copperfield Church, Houston, Texas

"If you find yourself confused on how God wants you to use the financial blessings he has given you, Bruce Miller's latest book, *Giving: The Three Questions*, offers a practical, biblical process to find the greatest impact for the kingdom and receive the joy in giving God wants for you."

Nick Ganter
Elder, Christ Fellowship, McKinney, Texas
Sr. Health Systems Executive for AbbVie

"Generosity drives spiritual growth and shakes us awake to where our resources truly come from, what we're supposed to do with what God gives us, and how we can love and bless the people he puts in our lives. You can always recognize a Christian by their fruits. Let this book be your launch into meaningful generosity."

Dr. Jennie Tissing, Ph.D.
Retired, Grants Administrator
Methodist Health System

"In my years consulting and advising CEO's throughout the U.S. and internationally, I've come to the simplest conclusion: there is a key difference between having wealth and being rich. Biblical giving is essential to having a rich and fulfilled life, but understanding what that means is essential as well. Bruce does a fantastic job outlining the reasons why, how and to whom all believers should be giving. The biblical lessons found within *Giving—The Three Questions* provide believers with the tools and knowledge to live out a rich and fulfilled life."

Seth Denson
Business & Market Analyst
National Media Contributor
Co-Founder of GDP Advisors

Giving

The Three Questions

Why give?

To whom?

How much?

Other books and studies by Bruce B. Miller

Shaken: When God Makes No Sense
A Fresh Look at Habakkuk

Big God in a Chaotic World
A Fresh Look at Daniel

Never the Same
A Fresh Look at the Sermon on the Mount

✥

Your Life in Rhythm
Your Life in Rhythm Study Guide

Your Church in Rhythm

The Leadership Baton
The Leadership Baton Group Study Guide
(written with Rowland Forman
and Jeff Jones)

**Leading a Church in a
Time of Sexual Questioning**
Grace-Filled Wisdom for Day-to-Day Ministry

Giving
The Three Questions

Why give?
To whom?
How much?

the WISDOM™
SERIES

Bruce B. Miller

Dadlin Media
— *wisdom for life* —

McKinney, Texas

Dadlin Media is the publishing imprint for Dadlin ministries, committed to illuminating wisdom to ignite people on fire for Jesus. See BruceBMiller.com for more resources.

ISBN: 978-1-68316-014-4

Printed in the United States of America
Unless otherwise noted, Scripture taken from the HOLY BIBLE, NEW INTERNATIONAL VERSION. Copyright © 1973, 1978, 1984, 2010.
International Bible Society.
Used by permission of Zondervan Publishing House.

2409 Rockhill, Rd.   McKinney, TX 75070

Dedication

I dedicate *Giving* to the greatest giver, God the Father, who gave the greatest gift, his one and only Son Jesus Christ, who gave his life for us.

Contents

Dedication   i

Contents   iii

Introduction   v

Chapter 1 Why give?   1

Chapter 2 To whom?   23

Chapter 3 How much?   45

Study Guide Introduction   69

Chapter 1 Study Guide - Why give?   79

Chapter 2 Study Guide - To whom?   95

Chapter 3 Study Guide - How much?   107

Final Thoughts   123

Acknowledgment   125

Recommended Resources   127

About the Author   129

Other Resources   133

Introduction

After raising five kids, I'm proud of my wife for going back to college later in life to earn a master's degree in Speech Language Pathology at Texas Women's University (TWU). In God's grace, Tamara secured a job even before she graduated. What this meant financially is that we were no longer paying for school, and we had a new income stream.

After hearing an inspiring message on God's generosity to us, Tamara and I were motivated to prayerfully reconsider our giving. It was such a blast to see how much more money we could give. We took the money we were paying for her tuition and re-directed it to our church's capital campaign. Then, from her new income, we increased our regular giving to our church's general ministries. And we set aside more money to give to others' needs that might come up the next year.

At the end of that year, we took some time to get away, just the two of us. We reserved a primitive cabin in an Oklahoma state park with a fireplace, and no Wi-Fi, which was a great place for us to unplug and reconnect with God and each other. During that time, we looked over our giving for the year and prayerfully decided to give extra gifts to the church, but it was December 30th—how would we do it?

We left the cabin and found a McDonald's in order to use their Wi-Fi so we could log on to the church's website and to our bank, so that we could give our extra gifts to the church. It was fun for us. It made us smile so big. We ended that year full of joy.

You may think we're nuts. For lots of people, giving is counter intuitive. Humanly, we reason, if I give $1,000 to the church, I will have $1,000 less.

That makes logical sense. But it's not the way God does math. We actually have more when we give money away. Jesus' teachings flip plenty of the world's "common sense" upside down.

The last is first
  (Matthew 19:30; Mark 10:31).

The servant is the greatest
  (Matthew 23:11).

When you lose your life, you save it
  (Matthew 16:25; Mark 8:35; Luke 9:24;
  17:33).

Giving money away makes you richer
  (2 Corinthians 8:1-3).

What it means to be richer ends up being much more than merely financial and the full blessings are only realized on a much longer timeline.

Many pastors avoid the topic of money because they are scared of your reaction. Among my pastor friends, we all know that the moment we broach money, we'll hear this well-worn complaint: "All this church cares about is money." Or its companion: "All this church talks about is money." Often these complaints come from people who don't faithfully give to the church. Rarely does a church only care about money, or talk about it more than the Bible does. And if that is happening, it's unhealthy.

The other reason pastors avoid this topic is because we don't want to be associated with the gross abuses out there. You've seen the stories about some pastor abusing their influence to buy an airplane or build a mansion. That kind of greedy, manipulative behavior drives me crazy and it makes God angry. No godly pastor wants anything to do with it. We did not enter the ministry to get rich.

My heart is to illumine biblical wisdom on generous giving so you can see what God wants you to do in this important arena of your life. I pray that you will be on fire for Jesus and this fire will be expressed in your giving.

Of course, generosity is broader than money, but most people's sincere questions relate to money. If you're already feeling tense, ask yourself why. Seriously. Giving is a spiritual issue that relates directly to following Christ, to growing in maturity. Jesus has a lot to say about money and material possessions. Check out the four gospels.

Let's knock out a few objections that might hinder you from hearing what God has for you.

Is Bruce writing this book to get more money for churches? My heart is not to get something *from* you, but rather to provide something *for* you. My desire is primarily for your spiritual growth, and for Christ's mission, not to get more money for a church budget or project.

Secondly, does Bruce benefit financially from this book? Sure, I could. And I have committed to give away at least 60 percent of any net profits.

Thirdly, couldn't you just donate your time instead of your money? It's good to volunteer and God wants you to do that but giving your time does not count for giving your money. Our money represents our very lives. It's a way God asks us to worship him.

In this arena of giving, people ask three common questions that I hope to answer. Rather than trying to get cute, I'm just putting them straight out:

1. Why should we give money?

2. To whom should we give?

3. And how much should we give?

These are honest, practical, important questions, for you, and for God.

Chapter 1

Why give?

It's a fair and obvious question. Why in the world should you give away your money?

- It's a limited resource.

- If you give it away, you have less.

- You never know what tomorrow holds. Who knows if you might lose your job or have an expensive medical issue or some other catastrophe?

- Longer-term, you need to worry about retirement.

- Whatever money you are not using today, you need to store away for your later years.

So it would be best to keep all the money you can.

Frankly, you need your money. And does the church really need it more than you do? You may wonder if your church is using the money responsibly. And if we get a bit more honest with ourselves, there's stuff we want to buy—a house, car, boat, motorcycle, phone, TV, dress or whatever.

Obviously, you can anticipate that I am going to say we should give generously, but why? There are wrong reasons to give:

- We should not give out of fear that God will punish us.

- We should not give to impress other people.

- We should not give to get.

Among all the people reading this book, imagine the wide spread of where people are on this topic. You may have never given to a church. You may have given not more than a few dollars or only sporadically. You may give with incredible generosity. Let's broaden the scope to your generosity in everyday life. Think about your giving to your family, to people in need, to global missions, to people in crisis, all the way to how much you tip people who serve you.

Our children are all generous. One of my sons is among the most generous people I know. He loves to give a tip so big it shocks the server. When we took Tamara out to dinner after her graduation from Texas Women's University, he bought appetizers for the whole table, four of them. After the main course, he bought four orders of sopapillas. Then he insisted on paying for the whole meal for everyone and added a big tip. That's lavish generosity. He loves giving. It brings him so much joy. His joy at Christmas comes from watching family members open the gifts he bought them.

Imagine if you were thrilled to give. Imagine if you were trying to figure out how to give as much as you could. And picture how you would feel if you gave like that. What could drive you to live that way?

Over our morning coffee on a Monday, I asked Tamara, "Why do you give?" By the way, Tamara is really good at giving. She said, "It's just fun. It brings me so much joy." She caught herself and said, "I wish my answer was deeper than that. It would sound more spiritual to say to please God or for eternal rewards or something like that," but she said, "Honestly, I just love to give." It brings her joy.

And it hit me, that's it. Giving creates joy. We should give because generosity creates joy. After talking to Tamara, I dove into the Bible to study how God's Word answers our question, Why give? My study verified Tamara's simple answer. We give because it creates joy.

Think back to your last Christmas presents. Can you remember the gifts you received? Now ask yourself if you can remember the gifts you gave.

For many people it is much easier to remember the gifts you gave because you spent time deciding what to buy, then you went shopping, made the purchase and wrapped the gift and watched the joy on the face of the one you love unwrapping it. Contrast your feelings as you opened your own gifts with your feelings as you watched ones you love opening the gifts you gave them.

While I had fun opening my gifts at Christmas, my greater joy was watching Tamara and my kids and grandkids open their gifts. What a blast to see little 10-month-old Amelia open her Daniel Tiger. And to see two-year-old Arabella thrilled with her multi-colored markers. It was my joy to give Tamara the weekender bag she wanted.

Giving makes us smile. Famous wealthy businessman Andrew Carnegie said, "Millionaires seldom smile."[1] Hoarding piles of money brings more trouble than it brings joy. It creates more frowns than smiles. Classic Christmas movies make this point—think of *Scrooge* or *The Grinch*.

Giving is contagious. It creates chain reactions of joy. Have you ever been with friends and seen what happens when one person starts laughing really hard, and then another person starts laughing and before you know it, everyone is laughing? It happens with yawns too. More fun is how smiles are contagious. You smile big and the person across from you can hardly stop from smiling. Giving creates smiles. My hope is that your God-inspired generosity creates a wave of smiles, a chain reaction of joy. Generous giving puts a smile on three faces. The first face is the most important. Generosity puts a smile on God's face.

1. Put a smile on God's face

Giving makes God happy. The Apostle Paul says in 2 Corinthians 9:7:

> *Each of you should give what you have decided in your heart to give, not reluctantly*

or under compulsion, **for God loves a
cheerful giver** (2 Corinthians 9:7).

When you give, you put a smile on God's face. This
may be because God himself is a cheerful giver, so
our generosity imitates God and it brings him joy
when we follow his model.

When you think about God, who God really is, you
want to please him. God is your creator. The triune
God, Father, Son and Holy Spirit is in a category of
one. There is none like him. God is incomparable.
And the one and only God tells us to give, to live
generous lives. He tells us to *excel in this grace of
giving* (2 Corinthians 8:7). I want to obey God
simply because he is God. God commands us *to be
rich in good deeds, and to be generous and willing
to share* (1 Timothy 6:18). Giving puts a smile on
God's face because giving obeys God, the creator of
everything.

My motivation to give comes not just from who
God is, but also from what he has done for us. You
give out of gratitude to God. God our Father is the

greatest giver who gave the greatest gift. The Bible says,

> *He who did not spare his own Son, but gave him up for us all—how will he not also, along with him, graciously give us all things?* (Romans 8:32).

If you have never trusted in Jesus Christ, that's the most important step you could take. God wants to give you eternal life, forgiveness for all your sins. He offers them to us in Jesus Christ. You receive his gift of salvation by placing faith in Jesus.

In God's Son, Jesus Christ, we have every spiritual blessing. Paul says,

> *Praise be to the God and Father of our Lord Jesus Christ, who has blessed us in the heavenly realms with every spiritual blessing in Christ* (Ephesians 1:3).

Your generous giving responds to his astoundingly previous generous giving. God has given you far more than you could ever give him.

And more than that, everything you have comes from him. In a sense, you own nothing. Every job, house, car and dollar ultimately comes from God who gives it to you to manage for him during your short stay on earth. You are a steward of his stuff. Like at the end of a Monopoly game, once your life ends, everything goes back in the box. All the properties, houses and hotels you owned, even Boardwalk, go back in the box. You don't take your money and possessions with you into the afterlife. You simply manage them while you are here.

In light of who God is and what God has done for you, you give to worship God. At Christ's birth, the Wise Men, the Magi, laid their generous gifts before baby Jesus. As a grown man, Jesus delighted in the widow who gave her two coins, all she had (Luke 21:1-4). He praised the unnamed woman who poured expensive perfume on his feet (Luke 7:36-50). Generous giving made Jesus smile.

It puts a smile on God's face. That's the most important smile.

In one of his parables, Jesus talked about a master who represents God. He praised his servant who managed his resources well. Imagine being the servant and having God say this to you:

> *Well done, good and faithful servant! You have been faithful with a few things; I will put you in charge of many things. Come and share your master's happiness!* (Matthew 25:21).

I love the thought of sharing in God's happiness. I want to hear him say to me, "Well done good and faithful servant." Generous giving puts that smile on God's face. By your giving, you can share in God's happiness. Giving creates joy, starting with God. The second smile is on others' faces. Generous giving puts a smile on others' faces.

2.   **Put a smile on others' faces**

Giving makes other people happy. It's such a joy to meet a need. When you give to someone in desperate need, you will often see not only a smile, but tears of joy.

One year over the Christmas holiday, a member of Christ Fellowship called asking if there was someone in need who they could anonymously help. What a joy one of our pastors had. You see there was another family in our church with a bunch of young kids who had a really hard year. This pastor had the privilege of delivering a large check to that family. Mom, dad, and their kids were filled with joy—smiles on every face. The prophet Isaiah poetically put it like this,

> *And if you spend yourselves in behalf of the hungry and satisfy the needs of the oppressed, then your light will rise in the darkness, and your night will become like the noonday* (Isaiah 58:10).

If we truly love God, then we will give generously to others in need. The Apostle John said it this way,

> *If anyone has material possessions and sees a brother or sister in need but has no pity on them, how can the love of God be in that person?* (1 John 3:17).

In fact, Proverbs says God will reward us,

> *Whoever is kind to the poor lends to the Lord, and he will reward them for what they have done* (Proverbs 19:17).

Giving to the poor is a way of giving to God. I love Jesus' story of the Good Samaritan who took care of a stranger and gave his money to pay for him to be taken care of. Image the smile on the face of that nameless stranger—and on the innkeeper's face who told him his bill was paid (Luke 10:25-37). And the smiles of everyone who heard about it.

In the early church, *they sold property and possessions to give to anyone who had need* (Acts 2:45). So, that the Bible records, *that there were no needy persons among them* (Acts 4:34–35). I would love to say that there were no needy people in Christ Fellowship because we all gave to anyone who has need.

It's a joy to give to those who are serving in ministry. A while back, Tamara and I got so much joy out of telling one of our Christ Fellowship global workers that we had decided to support them on a monthly basis. They thanked us and thanked us and thanked us. We didn't do it for the thanks. Our joy was to see the smile it put on their faces.

Paul commended the Macedonian Christians because *they urgently pleaded with us for the privilege of sharing in this service to the Lord's people* (2 Corinthians 8:4). They were eager to be involved in the privilege of financially supporting ministry to others. It's a blast to participate in what God is doing. When you get to share in God's work in Uganda, China or in your local community, it's a blast.

When you give to the church, you support all the staff. In speaking of those paid by the church, the Bible says a worker deserves his wages (1 Timothy 5:17–18.) Your giving pays their salaries and provides them with insurance. You put a smile on the face of every staff person.

Listen to how Paul summarizes the joyous impact of generous giving:

> *This service that you perform is not only supplying the needs of the Lord's people but is also overflowing in many expressions of thanks to God* [it puts a smile on God's face]. *Because of the service by which you have proved yourselves, others will praise God* [it puts a smile on others' faces] *for the obedience that accompanies your confession of the gospel of Christ, and for your generosity in sharing with them and with everyone else. And in their prayers for you*

their hearts will go out to you (2 Corinthians 9:12–14).

Generous giving puts a smile on God's face and on others' faces. Then there is one more smile. I was surprised that there seems to be more in the Bible about this smile than about the other two. It puts a smile on your own face.

3. Put a smile on your face

Giving makes you smile. The point is not that we give to get. Certainly not. We don't give to get rich. But passage after passage in the Bible teaches that giving brings you blessing. It brings you joy. It makes you smile. Listen to the Word of God as you read a few.

Here's the prophet Malachi:

> *"Bring the whole tithe into the storehouse, that there may be food in my house. Test me in this," says the LORD Almighty, "and see if I*

will not throw open the floodgates of heaven and pour out so much blessing that there will not be room enough to store it" (Malachi 3:10–12).

It's not that God brings you a little blessing, a dribble. No, he promises to open up the floodgates of heaven and pour out so much blessing you will not have room to store it. Proverbs says,

Honor the LORD with your wealth, with the firstfruits of all your crops; then your barns will be filled to overflowing, and your vats will brim over with new wine (Proverbs 3:9–10).

Notice again the abundance—filled to overflowing, brimming over.

This teaching continues in the New Testament. Listen to Jesus in the book of Luke:

Give, and it will be given to you. A good measure, pressed down, shaken together and running over, will be poured into your lap. For with the measure you use, it will be measured to you (Luke 6:38).

He refers to the ancient grain merchant who would fill the lap of his customer as full as possible until the grain ran over the edge. You can never out give God. The more you give, the more blessing he gives back.

Paul quoted Jesus making the basic point that giving brings joy. In Acts we read,

Remembering the words the Lord Jesus himself said: "It is more blessed to give than to receive" (Acts 20:35).

Let me paraphrase it. It brings more joy to give money than to receive money. It puts a bigger smile on your face to give than it does to receive. We give because generosity creates joy for God, for others and for us.

The blessings we receive are not only intrinsic to the act of giving itself, but also more blessings come from God when we give. God will enrich us in every way. Speaking of generous giving Paul says,

> *And God is able to bless you abundantly, so that in all things at all times, having all that you need, you will abound in every good work…. Now he who supplies seed to the sower and bread for food will also supply and increase your store of seed and will enlarge the harvest of your righteousness. You will be enriched in every way so that you can be generous on every occasion, and through us your generosity will result in thanksgiving to God* (2 Corinthians 9:7–11).

These blessings, these "riches," are much more than financial. Giving grows your soul. Generosity cures greed. Generous giving frees you from the grip of consumerism. It helps you let loose of this world and live for eternity. It helps you take your eyes off yourself and put your eyes on others.

Generous giving builds your faith as you tangibly express that your security is not in your savings but in your Savior.

Randy Alcorn wrote, "Giving is not God's way of raising money—it's his way of raising children."[2] Giving is part of spiritual maturity, part of following Jesus. Jesus said, *For where your treasure is, there your heart will be also* (Matthew 6:21). Giving grows your heart.

These blessings are not only here on earth, but also in heaven. They are now and they are eternal. Jesus said,

> *Do not store up for yourselves treasures on earth, where moths and vermin destroy, and where thieves break in and steal. But store up for yourselves treasures in heaven, where moths and vermin do not destroy, and where thieves do not break in and steal* (Matthew 6:19–20).

Paul said that by generous giving, we lay up treasures for the coming age, *so that they may take hold of the life that is truly life* (1 Timothy 6:17–19).

Giving brings you joy today and forever. Our smiles will be even bigger in heaven. It's been said that you brought nothing into the world and will take nothing out, but a deeper truth is that you can send treasure ahead. Your giving today stores up treasure in heaven. Many people miss this. What you do with your money today impacts eternity.

This saying from Proverbs summarizes the point:

> *One person gives freely, yet gains even more; another withholds unduly, but comes to poverty. A generous person will prosper; whoever refreshes others will be refreshed* (Proverbs 11:24–25).

Why give? Giving creates joy. You should give because it puts a smile on three faces: God's, others' and your own. Give generously to create waves of smiles, a chain reaction of joy. What might that look like? Give generously and watch the smile grow on the face of the other person, feel the smile spread across your face and picture God on his throne in heaven smiling as he watches you give.

Let's create a joy chain reaction, a wave of smiles.

Chapter 2

To whom?

On Monday, your Facebook feed shows you tragic pictures of a cute 6-year-old girl with bone cancer, and an old friend from high school is asking you to donate.

Your email box has two requests from Christian organizations sharing the latest urgent needs from the famine in Ethiopia, and the plight of young teenage girls being sex trafficked in Thailand.

The same day, two newsletters come by snail mail with an appeal for giving to a scholarship fund for your alma mater, and another to your local food bank.

Meanwhile, your local church receives an offering every Sunday. Your wife's brother who is a single dad, lost his job, and his severance ran out, so he and his two kids need help with basic needs.

On top of these giving opportunities, one of your college roommates serves as a missionary in India, and you agreed to support him on a monthly basis, but you also want to sponsor a needy child in a third-world country which requires a monthly financial commitment.

Sound familiar? Most of us are inundated with requests from charities and good causes to the point that it can be overwhelming. Requests come from the big organizations, such as the Red Cross, and from good causes, such as curing breast cancer. And often someone you know is involved. My daughter-in-law worked for St. Jude Children's Research Hospital. Crowd-funded appeals and the latest disaster compete for our charitable giving.

It can be confusing as to where you should give your money. How do you make wise choices for where to invest your giving dollars? My hope is to give you biblical clarity about divine priorities for your giving.

Three Basic Criteria

Three criteria apply to all giving opportunities. The first criterion is integrity. You should only give to organizations who have integrity. Sadly, some people use charitable causes to get rich. There are scams out there. Check if the head of the organization has an exorbitant salary, lives in a mansion or is buying private planes. See if there is an external audit or approval from an outside accrediting organization such as the EFCA (the Evangelical Council on Financial Accountability).

Secondly, you should give to organizations that are effective. Check out how a group or organization is using the money. Are they actually doing the good work they claim to do? See if they publish a report that shows their results. If you can do so, visit the organization or the area in which they are serving to see what's really happening.

Thirdly, look for transparency. At Christ Fellowship, we are committed to the highest integrity and effectiveness. And we are transparent with our finances. You, along with anyone in the world, can go to the Christ Fellowship website, www.cfhome.org. Click on "Giving." Scan down and you will see the same monthly report that goes to our Elder Board, then you can check out links to our financial policies, procedures and budget. We also post our annual external audit. We are open with our finances.

Good organizations have policies such as ones that guard against conflict of interest, that require double signatures on checks, and that limit who has access to a credit card.

At Christ Fellowship, every dollar is committed to our mission of being people helping people find and follow Christ, and we stretch each dollar. We are frugal. Every year when our auditor meets with the Elders, he compliments the Christ Fellowship finance team for having among the best practices of any church they audit.

Knowing you should give to organizations that have high integrity, effectiveness, and transparency, are there places God would have you prioritize in your giving? To whom should you give? There are three places that have biblical, divine priority. The first is to your church family.

1. To your church family

In the Old Testament, before the founding of the church, God's people were to support the temple, including providing for the priests and Levites who served in the temple. The priests and temple workers would be roughly equivalent to church staff today.

In the New Testament, over 90 percent of the references to "church" (in Greek, *ekklesia*) are to local, visible organized communities of people.

The book of Acts records the founding and multiplying of local churches. There were no parachurch ministries, no schools, mission agencies or radio ministries. The biblical passages on giving are written to local churches, such as the church in Corinth.

Consider the nature of the local church. Biblically, the church is the family of the Father, the body of Jesus Christ the Son, and the temple of the Holy Spirit. It is not simply one more non-profit organization created by humans. Rather, the church is a divine entity like marriage and family. Other good ministries and organizations are not parallel to the church nor do they replace the church. Churches are supernatural. So local churches today are divine organisms who are God's primary expression of his kingdom. And as such, your local church deserves priority in your financial giving.

The church is your spiritual family. Giving should start with your family. Every member in a healthy family contributes to the family. And rightly, you put family first.

Further, the Bible makes it clear that you have a responsibility to financially support those who teach, lead and care for you in local churches. To the Galatians, Paul writes,

> *Nevertheless, the one who receives instruction in the word should share all good things with their instructor* (Galatians 6:6).

And he gave direction to Timothy for the church in Ephesus,

> *The elders who direct the affairs of the church well are worthy of double honor* [a reference to financial support], *especially those whose work is preaching and teaching. For Scripture says, "Do not muzzle an ox while it is treading out the grain," and "The worker deserves his wages"* (1 Timothy 5:17–18).

Let me just confess that it is awkward to make this point as one who serves as a pastor in a local church, but it's the truth. Biblically, if you are being ministered to by church staff, you should financially support them so they can devote their time to teach and care for you and your children.

After extensive study on giving, in one of the most well-regarded books on the topic, author Gene Getz concludes, "The local church should be God's primary context for both systematic giving and maintaining accountability in the area of material possessions."[3] He advises, "A good rule of thumb is for Christians to give at least 10 percent of their income to their local churches before they support additional ministries."[4] Christian author Randy Alcorn says similarly, "Normally, I believe, the firstfruits, or tithe, should go directly to the local church."[5] Whether the amount is 10 percent or not, I agree with Getz and Alcorn that the biblical priority is to give to your local church as your spiritual family. The second biblical priority is to give to those in need.

2. **To those in need**

You see God's special heart for those in need in both the Old and New Testaments. He has special concern for orphans, widows and the oppressed. Proverbs affirms,

> *Those who give to the poor will lack nothing, but those who close their eyes to them receive many curses* (Proverbs 28:27).

- People in our church family

Of all those in need, our responsibility first is to those in our own church family. The parable of the sheep and the goats speaks to fellow believers. At the final judgment, the King will separate the people as a shepherd separates sheep and goats based on how a person met the needs of the least of our brothers and sisters. Jesus said,

Then the King will say to those on his right, "Come, you who are blessed by my Father; take your inheritance, the kingdom prepared for you since the creation of the world. For I was hungry and you gave me something to eat, I was thirsty and you gave me something to drink, I was a stranger and you invited me in, I needed clothes and you clothed me, I was sick and you looked after me, I was in prison and you came to visit me." Then the righteous will answer him, "Lord, when did we see you hungry and feed you, or thirsty and give you something to drink? When did we see you a stranger and invite you in, or needing clothes and clothe you? When did we see you sick or in prison and go to visit you?" The King will reply, "Truly I tell you, whatever you did for one of the least of these brothers and sisters of mine, you did for me" (Matthew 25:31–40).

In the book of Acts, we read about how the first church lived out what Jesus asked:

For there was no one needy among them, because those who were owners of land or houses were selling them and bringing the proceeds from the sales and placing them at the apostles' feet. The proceeds were distributed to each, as anyone had need (Acts 4:34–35).

The believers gave to the church and the church distributed funds to those in need. There was no one needy among them. We want the same reality in our local churches today. If anyone in a local church lacks daily food, adequate clothes or a place to live, we take care of each other. Of course, a church should perform due diligence to ensure the needs are legitimate and that the help is truly helping, not enabling.

Your church likely has a benevolence fund. At Christ Fellowship, our "Love Fund" is our fund to care for those in need in our church family first, and then those in our community in need. We distribute 100 percent of those funds directly to people as we verify the need, and help them to thrive long-term financially and spiritually. Not only do we give to people in need in our church family, but we also support people in our community.

- People in our community

Among the many proverbs about giving to the needy, Proverbs 19:17 gives a promise:

> *Whoever is kind to the poor lends to the LORD, and he will reward them for what they have done* (Proverbs 19:17).

Jesus makes this truth come alive in his story of the Good Samaritan. You may remember that a nameless man was attacked, beaten and robbed, then left on the side of the road. While a priest and a Levite passed by on the other side of the road, an everyday Samaritan took care of the hurt man. At the end of the story Jesus asked,

> *"Which of these three do you think was a neighbor to the man who fell into the hands of*

robbers?" The expert in the law replied, "The one who had mercy on him." Jesus told him, "Go and do likewise" (Luke 10:36–37).

The Bible calls us to show financial mercy to people in need in our community, including those of different ethnicities and beliefs.

It's a joy to help people in our local community. The people of Christ Fellowship have done food drives, bought Christmas Angel Tree gifts, repaired homes, and much more. One home that needed repair ended up becoming a much bigger project that took months and far more money than we anticipated. Members of the church took an interest in the homeowner and when he was losing his eyesight, they took him to doctor appointments and have helped in many practical ways, perhaps most of all by being faithful friends.

In December a few years ago, a tornado brought disaster to our community including two families in Blue Ridge, a town in the county in which we live. The Santillano's mobile home was shredded, but much worse, their three-day old, newborn little girl was killed. In addition, the Gonzalez family of nine, including a special needs girl lost their home and vehicles. Two leaders from Christ Fellowship, Bob and Terry, worked with a group of churches and agencies to verify needs and bring help. Immediate needs for food and clothing were covered, but both families needed a place to live.

Through people's generosity, we were able to provide two new manufactured homes fully furnished! I had so much joy being there to see their smiles and tears when the families walked in the door of their new homes for the first time.

Giving brings so much joy! It starts a cascade of joy, a chain reaction of smiles. There is a third biblical priority for where we should give. In addition to your local church and to those in need, we should prioritize giving to global missions.

3. To global missions (Propempo)

The gospel of Jesus Christ is the only hope for each one of us. It is the most important message. The Apostle Paul wrote,

> For what I received I passed on to you as of first importance: that Christ died for our sins according to the Scriptures (1 Corinthians 15:3).

The gospel shares the way anyone is saved eternally.

Jesus said that his followers are to be witnesses to the entire world, to the ends of the earth. To do that, we must go and send people to bring the message. In the book of Romans, we read,

> For, "Everyone who calls on the name of the Lord will be saved." How, then, can they call on the one they have not believed in? And how can they believe in the one of whom they have not heard? And how can

*they hear without someone preaching to
them? And how can anyone preach unless
they are sent? As it is written: "How
beautiful are the feet of those who bring
good news!"* (Romans 10:13–15).

When you give to global workers (missionaries),
you invest in the gospel.

This is a biblical model. In the four gospels, you
can see that people financially supported Jesus
and his disciples. This model continues with the
apostles. People in the churches sent out
missionaries (global workers) with financial
assistance.

One Greek word is used seven times in the New
Testament with a specific focus on giving to
missionaries. The word is *propempō*. It means to
assist someone in making a journey, to *send on
one's way* with food and money. *Propempō* became
an early Christian term that was used to exhort,
compel and even command believers to send
individuals or teams of gospel workers on their

way with all the needed resources to make their journey a success.

In 3 John, John writes a personal letter to a believer named Gaius, who had recently funded a team of visiting missionaries. John encouraged him to continue his funding,

> Please _send them on their way [propempo]_ in a manner that honors God. It was for the sake of the Name that they went out, receiving no help from the pagans. We ought therefore to show hospitality to such people so that we may work together for the truth (3 John 6b–8).

This giving to global workers is a biblical command to _propempo_, to financially assist those who are going to bring the gospel to the world. When you give to them, you become partners with them.

Here's the bottom line. Why do we give? To create joy. Remember the three smiles: on God's face, others' faces and your own face. Where should we give? Remember the three recipients: the church family, those in need and global workers.

Other Giving Priorities

Given that these are God's three priority recipients for our giving, how are we to consider other charitable opportunities such as to our university's scholarship fund, the Red Cross, and the American Heart Association? What about giving to personal crises such as the little girl with cancer? Needs such as these fall under the broad biblical direction that we are to do good to all. The Apostle Paul writes this advice to the believers in Galatia,

> *Therefore, as we have opportunity, let us do good to all people, especially to those who belong to the family of believers* (Galatians 6:10).

So on top of giving first to your local church, and then to those in need and to global missions, you should also take the opportunity to do good beyond that. Often this kind of giving aims at the second priority of giving to those in need.

My wife and I regularly give to our local food bank, especially when they offer double or triple matching for our gifts. We have given to a GoFundMe account for a friend with cancer. These tend to be smaller gifts for us and not as regular. The instruction to do good *especially* to those who belong to the family of believers encourages you to focus on personal relationships. Before giving to someone you do not know whether in your community or around the world, give to someone you know personally, especially if they are in your church.

What about giving to people in your own family who have fallen on hard times? Sometimes older parents have not saved enough to provide for their needs later in life. Also, sometimes young adults fail to launch well or make early costly mistakes. The Apostle Paul gave this instruction to his associate Timothy for the Christians in Ephesus,

> *But if a widow has children or grandchildren, these should learn first of all to put their religion into practice by caring for their own family and so repaying their parents and grandparents, for this is pleasing to God.... Anyone who does not provide for their relatives, and especially for their own household, has denied the faith and is worse than an unbeliever* (1 Timothy 5:4, 8).

However, this instruction does not mitigate your obligation to put priority on giving to your church, to those in need and to global missions. Taking care of your family is in a different category of financial stewardship. For instance, putting food on the table for your kids is not "giving" to them but carrying out part of your fundamental responsibility to provide for your family. In other words, it would be wrong to say to yourself, "I'm giving money to my mother-in-law to pay her rent, so I'm not going to give money to the church."

Our generous giving responds to God's prior and overwhelming generosity to us. God is the greatest giver who gave the greatest gift, his one and only Son. Giving worships God, honoring him as the incomparable triune God. Giving expresses gratitude to God for his uncountable gifts to us, so many spiritual blessings and life eternal. Giving is fun. It's a blast. Giving blesses others. It meets needs and advances the gospel. Giving makes an eternal investment and eternal difference. Giving blesses you. It will bring you joy as you bring others joy and, most importantly, it brings God joy. That's the generosity effect, a cascade of smiles, a joy chain reaction.

And to whom do you give to experience this joy? We discovered three biblical priorities for our giving:

1. To our church family

2. To those in need

3. To global workers

Chapter 3

How much?

Where does this question come from? It varies.

The question arises from sincere Christians who are not sure what the Bible says, but they really want to honor God.

Others ask the question out of a desire to find the minimum level. Their real question is, "How little could I give, and it still be acceptable?"

The question arises as we set personal budgets and prayerfully ask how much to spend, save and give. Concrete financial realities complicate the question, such as should I give if I am in debt? What if I am not able to pay my bills right now? What if I lost my job, but still have investments? What if I am on a fixed income? And more questions related to your specific financial circumstances.

Many Christians have been taught to "tithe," which is to give 10 percent. You may wonder if you should give 1/10th of your income, and then is that figured from your gross or your net, and what counts as income? If your grandma gives you $100 for your birthday, are you obligated to give $10 to your church?

You may have heard a slogan such as "give til it hurts" or "give more than you can afford." Is your giving ever enough? Jesus told one man in the Bible to give away all his money (Luke 18:22). And a widow who gave away all she had to live on was commended by Jesus (Mark 12:41-44). Is that the biblical standard for how much to give if you are really committed to God?

Why do you think the question of how much to give is so sensitive? Why do people avoid a conversation on giving? I wonder if it's because money ties straight to our hearts. What we do with our money concretely reveals our hearts. Jesus said,

> *Where your treasure is, there your heart is also* (Matthew 6:21).

It's a matter of the heart. Money concretely expresses what matters to us. It shows where our faith lies, and it is countable and objective, so it is sensitive.

Since your giving is a response to God's generosity, how much did he give? He gave his one and only Son. You could never "repay" God, and that's not even a noble motive for giving. We delight in God's amazing generosity to us that inspires us to be generous out of gratitude. God welcomes us into his family and offers us an eternal inheritance that believers share with Jesus Christ as coheirs. Our divine inheritance is simply incredible, so rich.

Let's cut through the rhetoric and go straight to God's Word to answer this practical, spiritual question. You do not want to be stingy, sporadic or unfaithful, but rather generous and honoring to God, and you want to avoid extremes, and avoid legalism. What does God's Word actually tell you about how much you should give?

The "Tithe"

One answer you will find to this question is to tithe. "Tithe" is one of those words you hear often in churches, but not much in general conversation. While the word *tithe* literally means "tenth," today the term "tithing" is often erroneously used of all giving. People talk about "tithing" $100 a month when they actually make $5,000 a month. A true tithe would be five times as much, $500, because that is 10 percent of $5,000.

Does God command you to give 10 percent? Good Christians disagree on this topic. Here's how I see it. In the Old Testament law, there were actually three "tithes"—a tithe was required to support the Levites, a second 10 percent was used for a religious festival, and every third year an additional 10 percent was collected for widows and orphans for a total of about 23 percent!

While Jesus refers to the tithe (Matthew 23:23), the New Testament never commands giving a tithe. However, the 10 percent guideline can serve as a simple starting point. For instance, even before the law, Abraham gave a tenth (Genesis 14:20). As we uncover New Testament principles for giving, you will see that many of us should be giving more than 10 percent or even 23 percent.

So, while the tithe is not a command or a law for Christians today, it is a simple, easy-to-figure guideline based on an historical precedent. I encourage parents to teach your children to give. When we gave our kids an allowance, we taught them to set aside 10 percent to give to the Lord at the church. If their allowance was $10 a week, they gave $1 a week, beginning a life of generosity.

If the answer is not that God requires a tenth (a tithe), then how much does the Bible say you should give? Given that you really want to honor God in this area of your life, what do you do? In spite of our varying financial circumstances, there are three biblical principles that can guide each one of us in deciding how much to give. To keep it simple, I call it "3P Giving." Each P stands for a guiding biblical principle. Your first P is Planned.

1. Planned

Generous giving is not haphazard, but prayerfully planned. On Sunday morning, you should not be determining how much you will give. That should have been determined ahead of time. Paul says,

> *Each of you should give what you have decided in your heart to give, not reluctantly or under compulsion, for God loves a cheerful giver* (2 Corinthians 9:7).

The word "decided" in Greek, *proērētai,* means to set aside beforehand, to decide in advance. Listen to Paul's direction to the Christians in Corinth:

On the first day of every week, each one of
you should set aside a sum of money (1
Corinthians 16:1).

You cannot set aside a sum of money without
planning in advance.

As you plan your giving, you should make giving
your first consideration before other allocations.
This is the firstfruits principle. Proverbs says:

Honor the LORD with your wealth, with the
firstfruits of all your crops; then your barns
will be filled to overflowing, and your vats
will brim over with new wine (Proverbs
3:9–10).

In an agrarian economy, the firstfruits were
literally the first of the crops of olives, wheat or
whatever they harvested. It would also be the
best. If they raised sheep, it would be the first and
best of their lambs. We are to give our first and
best to the Lord.

When we delay giving, we often forget to give, or the money gets used for something else. Some people add up all their financial obligations and then give on what is left. Or you may just look at what's left at the end of the month.

The better way is to plan it off the top. Take your income, calculate 10 percent or more and give it first, then allocate the rest to everything else. Plan to give to God first. You will find that your 90 percent goes further than your 100 percent when you honor God with your "firstfruits" by giving him the first 10 percent or more.

So how do you practically plan your giving? Some of you are more detailed planners with your money and some are more free spirits. In any case, you need to prayerfully determine your giving in advance. Take time to calculate your income, then set a percentage to give. My wife, Tamara, and I use Mint.com for our personal budgeting. If you are not sure where to start, I recommend 10 percent. If you can't get there all at once, make 10 percent your goal and start somewhere above zero. Start with 1 percent.

In general, I recommend giving at the same frequency you are paid or receive income. If you are paid weekly, give weekly. I'm paid a bi-monthly paycheck on the 10th and 25th, so my wife and I have set up our online giving in that rhythm.

If you are married, your giving is more complicated because you need to agree. If you are single, give all you want. That's one of the benefits of being single!

Husbands and wives rarely agree at the start. A conversation about giving can be a great way to grow your marriage with a spiritual conversation. I encourage you to set aside unhurried time, pray, then listen deeply to each other. Look at the financial facts for your family, pray for unity and then come to agreement. In general, I would lean toward the more generous spouse. That's what Tamara and I try to do with our giving decisions.

The first P in 3P Giving is Planned. The second P is Proportionate.

2. Proportionate

You can find this truth as far back as Moses in Deuteronomy.

> Each of you must bring a gift **in proportion** to the way the LORD your God has blessed you (Deuteronomy 16:17).

In his instructions to the Corinthians about their giving, Paul says,

> Now finish the work, so that your eager willingness to do it may be matched by your completion of it, **according to your means**. For if the willingness is there, the gift is acceptable **according to what one has, not according to what he does not have** (2 Corinthians 8:10–12).

Notice your giving is not based strictly on income, but on how the Lord has blessed you, according to what you have. This is broader than income.

Having said that, you may have very little or even nothing. If you are in deep poverty, your church family should come around you to help you. Let them know. They may not be aware of your situation. No member of a local church should go without basic needs for food, clothes and shelter. The rest of the church family is ready to give to you.

Your giving is to be in proportion to how you have been blessed by God. To the Corinthians, Paul said they were to set aside a sum of money *in keeping with your income* (1 Corinthians 16:2). He commended the amazingly generous Macedonian Christians for their model because, *they gave as much as they were able, and even beyond their ability* (2 Corinthians 8:3).

Most of us in the western world have been blessed financially far beyond the majority of people in the world and yet our giving is terribly disproportionate to our income. You can go on the Internet and find websites where you can compare your income to the rest of world. It's embarrassing, because at least for me, I had to stare at the fact that my income puts me in the top 1 percent of the world.

In a study of data from IRS tax returns, Scott Burns, a financial writer for the *Dallas Morning News,* discovered an alarming trend. Households with less adjusted gross incomes gave a much higher percentage to charity than those with higher adjusted gross incomes. At the low end, households with adjusted gross incomes of $10,000 to $15,000 gave an average of 11.6 percent. Households with adjusted gross incomes of $200,000 to $500,000 gave 2.5 percent.

Burns says if you study the entire table, you find that "Giving and income are inversely related. People with higher incomes give less."[6]

This phenomenon is the opposite of the biblical principle. As your income increases, your giving should increase. Generous giving is proportionate. Many Americans can give more than 10 percent and still handle other obligations responsibly. Let's look at the actual giving for a church. This data comes from my own church several years ago based on annual giving. And I'm told these percentages are common in American churches.

1. 16 percent of the households gave over $4,000 with an average gift of $9,508.
2. 29 percent gave between $400 and $3,999 with an average gift of $1,596.
3. 20 percent gave $1 to $399 with an average gift of $122.
4. 35 percent of households gave zero.

Try to find yourself on the list. Into which category did you fall last year in terms of giving to your own local church? Of course, the amount of your income makes a big difference in the amount of your giving. One problem is that as our income increases, our spending increases, but too often our giving does not increase.

Let's get practical. Figure out what percentage of your income you gave last year. Look at your last paycheck for the year or your
W-2. Or just look at your income last month, and the percentage of your income that you gave last month.

Honestly face the truth about your giving in terms of the percentage of your income. One couple in our church really impressed me. They did this exercise and confessed they did not feel good about their giving and wanted to be held accountable. So they gave me an envelope with a copy of the page from their 1040 tax return that lists their adjusted gross income and a copy of their contribution statement from the church. Then they wrote the percentage of their giving to the church. The first year it was something like 2.8 percent, but over the next two years, they have given me the same envelope, and every year the percentage has grown.

Once you figure out what proportion you are giving today, take a step forward. Take one step up from 3 percent to 4 percent. Or from 10 percent to 11 percent or up to 25 percent or even 50 percent. One family in our church gave 50 percent of their income and they loved it. You can't out give God.

If you have any income at all and are giving nothing, I encourage you to start with something. If are you giving something, I encourage to pray about 10 percent. Make a big faith jump. If you are at 10 percent, I encourage you to pray about a step beyond that.

But what if you are in debt? Should you pay off your debt before you start giving? No. Give first. Honor God above your creditors. What if you are barely paying bills? Give something anyway. Take a hard look at where your money is going, especially in discretionary areas such as clothing, eating out, entertainment, including cable and satellite TV, and your cell phone plan. Your giving may not be 10 percent of your income, but give more than zero.

Giving is one of the only areas where God invites you to test him. I invite you to take God up on his invitation in Malachi, where God says,

> "Bring the whole tithe into the storehouse, that there may be food in my house. Test me in this," says the Lord Almighty, "and see if I will not throw open the floodgates of heaven and pour out so much blessing that there will not be room enough to store it" (Malachi 3:10).

I've encouraged many people to take this "Malachi Challenge" and no one has ever regretted it. God keeps his promise. The blessings may not be financial. They might be better than money.

How much should you give? Your giving should be Planned and Proportionate. Those are the first two Ps. Here's the third. Our giving should be Progressive.

3.   Progressive

Most of us want to keep growing in faith, knowledge and love. We want to take next steps to move further down the path to Christ-likeness. Yet in regard to generous giving, many decide a fixed percentage or level giving amount and stay there for life. But spiritual maturity includes growing in generous giving. Paul tells us,

> But just as you excel in everything—in faith, in speech, in knowledge, in complete earnestness and in your love for us[1]—see that you also excel in this grace of giving (2 Corinthians 8:7).

To excel, in Greek, *perisseuete*, means to abound, to be outstanding. You do not want to be stagnant in your giving. You should excel in the grace of giving. You may have heard of prayer warriors, people who are amazing at prayer. What about giving warriors? God has entrusted us with so much. Generous givers progress in their giving.

---

[1] Some manuscripts *in our love for you*

One member of our church agreed to let me share his story. Here it is.

> "I hope this encourages everyone to enjoy the blessings of giving and generosity. I have had 4 major milestones in my giving and generosity. Years ago as a new believer with a young family, God led me to know that if I was really going to trust Him, I would have to trust Him with the first 10 percent. Amazingly, we got through those lean years without going into debt while staying in the black.

> "Several years later, I was impressed by a sermon about not just giving, but giving gladly and beyond the tithe. We started giving a greater percentage and each time we got more, we gave more.

> "Then about four years ago, we started to give without being so concerned about the tax deduction. More giving went directly to individuals as needs arose. One year ago,

we set out to give more by trying to say yes each time a need arose at church or in the ministries we support. It was a great blessing to meet needs throughout the year. We have been blessed and we are confident that God will bless your giving efforts."

Paul motivated the Corinthian Christians by sharing the example of the believers in Macedonia. They still inspire me today to progress in my generosity. In 2 Corinthians chapter 8 Paul writes:

Now we make known to you, brothers and sisters, the grace of God given to the churches of Macedonia, that during a severe ordeal of suffering, their abundant joy and their extreme poverty have overflowed in the wealth of their generosity. For I testify, they gave according to their means and beyond their means (2 Corinthians 8:1–3).

They gave beyond what could be reasonably expected of them. Even in an ordeal of suffering, which may have been a famine, in their extreme poverty they overflowed in rich generosity and abundant joy. They gave not just according to their means, but beyond their means!

Over the years, I've been quietly praying that I could follow the example of R.G. LeTourneau, for whom the university is named. LeTourneau excelled in generosity. As an inventor of earthmoving machines, LeTourneau reached the point of giving 90 percent of his income to the Lord. As he put it, "I shovel out the money, and God gives back more. God has a bigger shovel." One day I hope to give 90 percent of my income. That would be awesome and so much fun.

Of course, the lady who many consider the greatest giver in the Bible, gave the least amount. Jesus held up a poor widow as an example of generous giving. In Luke 21 we read,

> *Jesus looked up and saw the rich putting their gifts into the offering box. He also saw a poor widow put in two small copper coins.*

He said, "I tell you the truth, this poor widow
has put in more than all of them. For they all
offered their gifts out of their wealth. But
she, out of her poverty, put in everything she
had to live on" (Luke 21:1–4).

These two copper coins would be worth today
about 58 cents each. She gave $1.16. Which is
larger, $1.16 or $11,600? Obviously $11,600, but
not to Jesus. While others gave out of their wealth,
she gave out of her poverty. It is not the number of
coins given, but the number of coins left over. The
disciples saw portions; Jesus saw proportion. The
disciples saw how much was given; Jesus saw how
much was left.

After you give, how much do you keep? In the
grace of giving, no one has an advantage. If you
have had a big decrease in your income, you may
have to decrease your giving, but you can still well
up in generosity. Regardless of your income, you
can be the biggest giver, not that that's the goal,
but you get the point.

What's in your heart when you ask the question: How much should I give? I believe God is calling each of us to grow to the place where we seek to give as much as we can. When you see the incredible generosity of God and the high stakes of the gospel, you are compelled.

Your giving funds the advance of the gospel that saves people eternally. One of the most famous and soul-stirring movies of the last few decades won seven Oscars. *Schindler's List* tells the story of businessman Oskar Schindler, who though initially motivated by profit, showed extraordinary courage and dedication to save the lives of Jewish people during the Holocaust. The scene at the end of movie is gripping, haunting. Although he had given a huge amount of his resources and made a massive impact, he says in tears with intense emotion, "I could have got more. I threw away so much money. I did not do enough." He pulls a gold pin off his jacket and says, "I could have sold it and saved one more person." (It's worth looking up the clip to watch it.)

May we be equally compelled. When you give to your local church, you impact children and students. Kids' lives are literally saved spiritually and physically—and you are changed in the process. Like Oskar Schindler, most of us look back on so much money we have wasted, money that could have been invested in saving lives with the gospel of Jesus.

Schindler wished he had given even more. The Scripture calls you to grow in generosity, to excel in the grace of giving. However, godly giving is not inspired by guilt, but by joy. When you give generously, you create joy. You put a smile on God's face. You put a smile on others' faces when you meet their physical needs and even more when you fund the gospel that saves them eternally. Giving brings blessings. It creates joy.

We have one simple question in this chapter: How much should I give? It turns out that as we grow spiritually, and realize how much God has given to us and how much joy we find in giving, the question changes from how much *should* I give to how much *can* I give? Biblically, generous giving is 3P Giving: Planned, Proportionate and Progressive. We plan our giving in proportion to what we have been given as we progress in greater and greater generosity.

Here's the bottom line:

> *Why do we give?*
> To create joy. Remember the three smiles.

> *To whom should we give?*
> Remember the three recipients: your church family, those in need and global workers.

> *How much do we give?*
> Remember the 3Ps of giving, Planned, Proportionate and Progressive.

Your generous giving responds to God's prior and overwhelming generosity to us. God gave the greatest gift, his one and only Son through whom we receive eternal life by trusting in him.

If you have never trusted in Jesus Christ, that's the most important step you could take. God wants to give you eternal life, forgiveness for all your sins. He offers them to us in Jesus Christ. You receive his gift of salvation by placing faith in Jesus. Then your giving imitates God. Giving brings you joy as you bring others joy and, most importantly, brings God joy. That's the generosity effect, a cascade of smiles, a joy chain reaction.

May you excel in the grace of giving creating a massive wave of joy!

Study Guide Introduction

This Study Guide will deepen your understanding and increase your spiritual growth. To enrich your growth, study with others so you can encourage and sharpen each other. We grow best in community.

The WISDOM Process© ™

As children of God living in a materialistic world, we need to learn how to think like Christ with biblical, spiritual wisdom for life.

Tested by thousands of people and hundreds of groups, the six-step WISDOM Process offers a surprisingly simple and profoundly powerful way to think. Today we are drowning in data and starving for wisdom. We Google for information on any topic, but we cannot find wisdom for life's complex challenges. This simple process can guide you to wisdom.

You will find that you can use The WISDOM Process not only in this Bible study but also for issues you face in ordinary life.

In order to accelerate your learning, this Study Guide employs The WISDOM Process. This process of thinking helps us move from knowing facts to transforming our lives in God's power. Most adults learn differently than children. Research into adult learning and studies of ancient education both show that people learn best when they have a reason to learn: a question to answer, a problem to solve or a mystery to unravel. All of us have these in our lives.

 **Pray**

Role of Prayer

We access the guidance of God's Spirit through prayer and the Word of God. While God wants us to use our minds to study his Word to gain his revealed life direction, the Bible tells us:

> *If any of you lacks wisdom, he should ask God, who gives generously to all without finding fault, and it will be given to him* (James 1:5).

Bible study should be covered with prayer. Paul prayed like this for the Colossians:

> *For this reason, since the day we heard about you, we have not stopped praying for you and asking God to fill you with the knowledge of his will through all spiritual wisdom and understanding* (Colossians 1:9).

In answer to your prayers, the Spirit will shape your desires and then you will develop the mind of Christ. Rather than prayer being a specific step in The WISDOM Process, it should be threaded throughout the process of your study from start to end.

You will find that as you pray, the Spirit of God will guide you to truth. As a group, if you will prayerfully listen to the Spirit, he will direct your conversation to deep spiritual wisdom, conviction and motivation to honor God in daily life choices.

W Work the issue: *What's really at stake*?

Prepare your heart and mind before engaging God's Word. Take a moment to pray about questions in your life and issues arising from the Scripture you are studying. Consider how the Lord may want to impact you at this time. Bring your questions to your study of God's Word.

I Investigate Scripture: *What does God say?*

God's Word is our authority for life. It is our guide for belief and behavior. Our lives must be grounded in the Word of God. It is our primary source of absolute, divine truth. Spend time prayerfully and carefully considering what the biblical text is saying.

S Seek counsel: *What do wise people say?*

After studying the Scripture for ourselves, it is wise to seek the counsel of others. In Proverbs, Solomon said there is wisdom in a multitude of counselors. Wise people listen to advice (Proverbs 12:15; 13:10; 19:20). We provide you with well-researched input in these chapters to help you understand God's Word better, but of course this counsel itself must be judged by the Word of God.

D Develop your response: *What do I think?*

We learn best when we actively engage. Writing down answers to questions will deepen your interaction with God's Word. Some questions are designed to increase your focus and understanding of the Scripture; others help you apply God's Word to your life.

O Openly discuss: *What do we think?*

Life transformation increases when we sharpen each other in dynamic discussion. You will grow more if you study with a group where you can wrestle together with how to understand and obey God's Word. Together, prepared people led by the Holy Spirit will generate a dynamic in which ideas and wisdom multiply beyond what any individual could produce.

M Move to action: *What will I do?*

Christ calls us to obey all he commands (Matthew 28:20). The point of Bible study is not simply knowledge, but obedience. We are studying God's Word to be more and more conformed to the image of Jesus Christ to grow to maturity. The Bible tells us that hearing the Word without acting on it is like building a house on sand, while acting on the truth is like building a house on rock (Matthew 7:24–27; James 1:22–25). We are in the business of building houses on the Rock! Our study should lead us to move to action in the Spirit's power.

Flow chart of
The WISDOM Process™

Work the Issue — What's really at stake?

Investigate Scripture — What does God say?

IT'S NOT CLEAR

IT'S CLEAR

Seek Counsel — What do wise people say?

Develop your Response — What do I think?

IT'S CLEAR

Move to Action — What will I do?

IT'S NOT CLEAR

Openly Discuss — What do we think?

Chapter 1 Study Guide

Why give?

NOTE: Each week you will work through the first few steps on your own. *Pray, Work the issue, Investigate Scripture* and *Develop your response.* Then when you meet with your group, you will discuss the questions in the *Openly discuss* step. Finally, after your group meeting, you will take the actions in the *Move to action* step.

 **Pray**

Prepare your heart and mind before engaging God's Word. Take a moment to pray about your personal questions, and questions over issues arising from the motivation for giving. Talk with God about your own struggles with why you should give.

W Work the issue: *What's really at stake*?

None of us knows our hearts. Motivations are mysterious and always mixed, never fully pure this side of heaven. Why do we fail to be more generous? What holds us back from giving? One way to gain insight into our question, "Why should we give?" can come from flipping the question into, "Why don't we give?"

Allow yourself to think deeply about your views on money and material possessions. How are our finances connected to our hearts? Ask God to help you see how our money relates to our relationship with him.

Giving ties to faith, to worship, to love, and contentment, as well as to idolatry, to fear and consuming.

What's at stake? What is the central issue or issues being addressed? What is the biggest issue for you?

Write down the main issue(s):

God's Word should guide our lives including our mindset about our money, and specifically how we view giving.

Read these verses slowly, even re-reading them several times, asking the Holy Spirit to transform your mindset on giving to become like Jesus' mindset.

▌**I** Investigate Scripture: *What does God say?*

The questions are designed to help you engage God in his Word. Use them to help you consider what God says to us.

1. *Each of you should give what you have decided in your heart to give, not reluctantly or under compulsion, for God loves a cheerful giver* (2 Corinthians 9:7).

    ▪ How does our giving impact God?

2. *Excel in this grace of giving* (2 Corinthians 8:7).

   Be rich in good deeds, and to be generous and willing to share (1 Timothy 6:18).

- Regarding giving, what does God command?

3. *He who did not spare his own Son, but gave him up for us all—how will he not also, along with him, graciously give us all things?* (Romans 8:32).

Praise be to the God and Father of our Lord Jesus Christ, who has blessed us in the heavenly realms with every spiritual blessing in Christ (Ephesians 1:3).

- How would you describe God's generosity in what he has given to us?

4. Paul commended the Macedonian Christians because *they urgently pleaded with us for the privilege of sharing in this service to the Lord's people* (2 Corinthians 8:4).

This service that you perform is not only supplying the needs of the Lord's people but is also overflowing in many expressions of thanks to God. Because of the service by which you have proved yourselves, others will praise God for the obedience that accompanies your confession of the gospel of Christ, and for your generosity in sharing with them and with everyone else. And in their prayers for you their hearts will go out to you (2 Corinthians 9:12–14).

- According to these passages, how does your giving impact other people?

5. *"Bring the whole tithe into the storehouse, that there may be food in my house. Test me in this," says the* Lord *Almighty, "and see if I will not throw open the floodgates of heaven and pour out so much blessing that there will not be room enough to store it"* (Malachi 3:10–12)

  ▪ What does God promise to those who give the "whole tithe?"

  ▪ What might it look like for you to "test" God in this way?

6. *Remembering the words the Lord Jesus himself said: "It is more blessed to give than to receive" (Acts 20:35).*

    And God is able to bless you abundantly, so that in all things at all times, having all that you need, you will abound in every good work.... Now he who supplies seed to the sower and bread for food will also supply and increase your store of seed and will enlarge the harvest of your righteousness. You will be enriched in every way so that you can be generous on every occasion, and through us your generosity will result in thanksgiving to God (2 Corinthians 9:7–11).

    ▪ In what ways you do experience more blessing when you give contrasted with when you receive?

7. *Do not store up for yourselves treasures on earth, where moths and vermin destroy, and where thieves break in and steal. But store up for yourselves treasures in heaven, where moths and vermin do not destroy, and where thieves do not break in and steal* (Matthew 6:19–20).

- How does our giving on earth have eternal impact?

S Seek counsel: *What do wise people say*?

Scan through chapter one looking for the main points and what really spoke to you. If you have time, check out answers to why we should give in one of the recommended resources beginning on page 127.

D Develop your response: *What do I think*?

1. What holds you back from giving more, more often?

2. How would you describe God's generous giving?

3. How does your giving impact God?

4. In what ways can your giving bring joy to others?

5. According to the Bible, how does your giving bless you?

6. In summary, how would you answer the question, why should you give?

◉ Openly discuss: *What do we think*?

[To be discussed with your group]

Financial giving is a sensitive subject that we are usually not comfortable talking about even with other Christians. Let's give each other permission to be open and authentic about this topic. Those who are strong in this area, please share how God has worked in your heart and life. Those who are weak in this area, be honest about your struggles. As the body of Christ, we can help one another grow to be more like Jesus.

1. What do you think makes giving such a sensitive topic? And why do people seem to avoid the topic, even in church Bible studies and small groups?

2. What holds you back from more generous giving?

3. How does giving put a smile on God's face? What about God motivates you to give generously (2 Corinthians 9:7; Romans 8:32; Ephesians 1:3; Matthew 25:21)?

4. How does generous giving put a smile on others' faces? Share stories of the joy you saw in someone else's face when you gave to them

(Isaiah 58:10; 1 John 3:17; Proverbs 19:17; Acts 4:34-35).

5. How does generous giving put a smile on your face? Read through some of God's promises: Malachi 3:10–12; Proverbs 3:9–10; Luke 6:38; Acts 20:35; and 2 Corinthians 9:7-11. Which of these impacts you the most, and why?

6. How can generous giving have an eternal impact (Matthew 6:19-20; 1 Timothy 6:17-19)?

7. Of all we've talked about, what motivates you to be more generous? And how are you feeling called to be more generous?

M Move to action: *What will I do?*

[To be acted on after your group discussion]

➢ Write out why you will give to God.

(The point is to crystallize your conclusions. Use the format that works for you, whether a paragraph or a set of bullet point phrases.)

➢ Go through your records and figure out the current amount you give in an average month. Then calculate what percentage that amount is of your income.
(The point is to face the reality of your current giving so you know from where you are starting.)

➢ If you are married, discuss why you give as a couple. If you have kids at home, involve them in the conversation.

Chapter 2 Study Guide

To whom?

 **Pray**

Divine wisdom comes from God's Spirit. Talk with God about to whom you should give. Ask God your questions regarding where you should direct your giving? Pray for the Holy Spirit to give insight into your specific situations and decisions.

W **Work the issue:** *What's really at stake*?

This question regarding to whom we should give surfaces our values and exposes our priorities. It's not simple to contrast giving to your family member with giving to the Red Cross with giving to your church. These days with social media, we are presented with more financial appeals than in previous times. How do we sort through all the opportunities?

If you are married, your giving priorities are likely not the same as your spouse's. Looking to God's Word can help you come to unity, at least on the overarching biblical priorities for where you send your giving.

Many people have never thought very hard about what kinds of organizations or needs should have priority in our giving decisions, but it's an important question to answer.

What's at stake? What is the central issue or issues being addressed? What is the biggest issue for you?

Write down the main issue(s):

▋ Investigate Scripture: *What does God say?*

1. God describes the church as his family. In fact, when you add up all the uses of brother and sister, "family" may be the most common image of the church in the New Testament.

   Therefore, as we have opportunity, let us do good to all people, especially to those who belong to the family of believers (Galatians 6:10).

   And in fact, you do love all of God's family throughout Macedonia (1 Thessalonians 4:10).

   - How does the truth that your local church is your spiritual family, guide the priority of your giving?

2. *Nevertheless, the one who receives instruction in the word should share all good things with their instructor* (Galatians 6:6).

    The elders who direct the affairs of the church well are worthy of double honor [a reference to financial support], *especially those whose work is preaching and teaching. For Scripture says, "Do not muzzle an ox while it is treading out the grain," and "The worker deserves his wages"* (1 Timothy 5:17–18).

    ▪ How do these two passages convey the priority of giving to your local church?

3. *Those who give to the poor will lack nothing, but those who close their eyes to them receive many curses* (Proverbs 28:27).

   Whoever is kind to the poor lends to the Lord, *and he will reward them for what they have done* (Proverbs 19:17).

   "Which of these three do you think was a neighbor to the man who fell into the hands of robbers?" The expert in the law replied, "The one who had mercy on him." Jesus told him, "Go and do likewise" (Luke 10:36–37).

   ▪ How would you contrast God's response to those who give to the poor with those who do not help them?

4. *Please <u>send them on their way [propempo]</u> in a manner that honors God. It was for the sake of the Name that they went out, receiving no help from the pagans. We ought therefore to show hospitality to such people so that we may work together for the truth* (3 John 6b–8).

- Given the importance of the gospel message, how does this passage show us the priority of giving to global missions?

S Seek counsel: *What do wise people say*?

Scan through chapter two looking for the main points and what challenged you. Identify questions you want to resolve. If you have time, look in one of the recommended resources beginning on page 127 to discover more insights into the question of to whom we should give.

D Develop your response: *What do I think*?

1. To whom are you currently giving? And to whom are you giving the most?

2. Why should your local church have priority in your giving?

3. What are other biblical priorities for where you direct your giving?

4. How does giving to good causes fit into your overall giving plan?

5. How does financially helping people in your family fit in your overall stewardship of your finances?

◉ Openly discuss: *What do we think?*

[To be discussed with your group]

1. What kinds of financial requests have you received in the last year? To what causes, organizations or groups do you typically give?

2. Why is your church family the top biblical priority for your giving (1 Corinthians 9:3-14; 1 Timothy 5:17-18)?

3. When we consider giving to those in need, who should we put first (1 John 3:17; James 2:14-16; Matthew 24:31-40; Acts 4:34-35)?

4. Why should we make giving to global missions a priority in our giving (Romans 10:13-15; 1 Corinthians 15:3; Matthew 10:9-10; 3 John 5-8; Titus 3:13-14; Romans 15:24; 1 Corinthians 16:6, 10-11)? What has been your experience in this area?

5. How does giving to good causes fit into our giving priorities?

6. How does financially helping members of our families fit in our overall giving plan?

7. How do you need to adjust to whom you give to be more in line with biblical priorities?

M Move to action: *What will I do?*

[To be acted on after your group discussion]

➢ Write down your giving priorities in terms of
  to whom you give.
  (The point of this exercise is to crystallize your
  conclusions to guide your giving decisions.)

➢ Examine your giving over the last year or so.
  Write down how much you have given to your
  church family, to the needy, and to missions.
  Then calculate how much you have given to
  other causes.

➢ Decide on any changes you will make to bring
  your giving plan more in line with biblical
  priorities. If you are married, discuss to whom
  you give, and if you have kids at home, include
  them in the conversation.

Chapter 3 Study Guide

How much?

 **Pray**

God promises to give wisdom to those who ask. He gives us the mind of Christ to see the Father's will. Talk with God about how much you should give. Ask the Holy Spirit for insight into your specific financial situation and giving decisions.

W **Work the issue:** *What's really at stake*?

If you have trusted in Jesus Christ, then on your best days you really do want to honor God with your giving. But how much giving will honor God?

If you are really giving in a mature manner, then how much money should you give?

Certainly, the Holy Spirit is involved in guiding us, but does God give us any guidelines to help? Can you ever give enough? Married couples often disagree over this question. One wants to give more and the other less.

What's at stake? What is the central issue or issues being addressed? What is the biggest issue for you?

Write down the main issue(s):

▐ Investigate Scripture: *What does God say?*

1. *Where your treasure is, there your heart is also* (Matthew 6:21).

   ▪ How does your giving connect with your heart? How could putting your treasure somewhere direct your heart?

2. *Each of you should give what you have decided in your heart to give, not reluctantly or under compulsion, for God loves a cheerful giver* (2 Corinthians 9:7).

   On the first day of every week, each one of you should set aside a sum of money (1 Corinthians 16:1).

- Notice the verbs, "decided" and "set aside." What is God telling us to do in regard to our giving? How could you practically do that these days?

3. *Honor the LORD with your wealth, with the <u>firstfruits</u> of all your crops; then your barns will be filled to overflowing, and your vats will brim over with new wine* (Proverbs 3:9–10).

- How would you describe the "firstfruits" principle to someone else?

4. *Each of you must bring a gift <u>in proportion</u> to the way the LORD your God has blessed you* (Deuteronomy 16:17).

    Now finish the work, so that your eager willingness to do it may be matched by your completion of it, <u>according to your means</u>. For if the willingness is there, the gift is acceptable <u>according to what one has, not according to what he does not have</u> (2 Corinthians 8:10–12).

    ▪ According to these passages, how much should you give to God?

5. *But just as you excel in everything—in faith, in speech, in knowledge, in complete earnestness and in your love for us[2]—see that you also excel in this grace of giving* (2 Corinthians 8:7).

Now we make known to you, brothers and sisters, the grace of God given to the churches of Macedonia, that during a severe ordeal of suffering, their abundant joy and their extreme poverty have overflowed in the wealth of their generosity. For I testify, they gave according to their means and beyond their means (2 Corinthians 8:1–3).

- How would God have us to grow in giving? Consider the model of the Macedonians. How were they a great model to other believers?

---

[2] Some manuscripts *in our love for you*

6. *Jesus looked up and saw the rich putting their gifts into the offering box. He also saw a poor widow put in two small copper coins. He said, "I tell you the truth, this poor widow has put in more than all of them. For they all offered their gifts out of their wealth. But she, out of her poverty, put in everything she had to live on"* (Luke 21:1–4).

- What impresses you about the poor widow's giving?

S Seek counsel: *What do wise people say?*

Scan through chapter three looking for the main points, for where you agree and where you disagree. Identify remaining questions you want to answer. If you have time, look in one of the recommended resources beginning on page 127 to find more insights into how much you should give.

D Develop your response: *What do I think?*

1. What is your current giving plan? (It may be that you don't yet have one.) What practical steps would you need to take to plan your giving in advance?

2. What is your view on "tithing"?

3. How would you answer another person who asked you, "How much does the Bible say we are to give?"

4. What is the current percentage of your income that you give to your local church? To all causes in total?

5. As you picture your future spiritual growth as a disciple of Jesus, how would like to grow in the grace of giving?

◉ Openly discuss: *What do we think?*

[To be discussed with your group]

1. What is a "tithe" and what does the Bible teach about tithing?

2. The Bible says to decide what to give in advance (2 Corinthians 9:7; 1 Corinthians 16:1), so what could we practically do in order to decide in advance what to give?

3. We are to give of our "firstfruits" (Proverbs 3:9-10). How could the "firstfruits" principle apply to current-day ways of receiving income?

4. We are to give proportionately (Deuteronomy 16:17; 2 Corinthians 8:3, 10-12; 1 Corinthians 16:2). If you are comfortable, share the current percentage of your income that you are giving to your local church, and the percentage to all places total. (Please feel no pressure to share your percentages. Many people prefer to stay confidential. I encourage you not to share specific amounts.) What steps could you take to give more in proportion to the way the Lord has blessed you financially?

5. Read the example of the Macedonians in 2 Corinthians 8:1-3. What impresses you about their model? Then read the story of the poor widow's generosity in Luke 21:1-4. What inspires you about the widow's giving?

6. Our generous giving should be progressively growing so we excel in the grace of giving (2 Corinthians 8:7). How has your giving grown over your lifetime? How do you hope it grows in the years ahead?

7. Review the whole series.

    a. Why do we give? (Remember the 3 smiles).
    b. To whom should we give? (Remember the 3 recipients).
    c. How much should we give? (Remember the 3Ps).

8. As a result of this study, what actions will you take so you excel in the grace of giving?

M Move to action: *What will I do?*

[To be acted on after your group discussion]

➢ Write down the amount of your giving over the last year, or few months. Then write down your income over that same period of time. Calculate the percentage of your income that you give. Be specific about what percentage you give to your local church, and what percent you give to everything else.

➤ Look at the "Generosity Ladder" to identify where your giving currently stands and where you want to be. Decide to take at least one step up the ladder. (You can see the Generosity Ladder on page 121.) Consider taking the "Malachai Challenge." See Malacahi 3:10-12. Give your tithe (10% of your income) to God through your local church for 90 days and see if you experience divine blessings.

➤ Look back over your "Move to Action" sections. Finalize your answers for yourself in terms of why you give, to whom you will give and how much you will give.

➢ Ask God to confirm in your heart any changes you should make in your giving, and make them.

GENEROSITY LADDER

Progressive

How much would God have me keep of God's stuff?
I regularly raise the amount of giving to our church.

Proportional

How much would God have me give of God's stuff?
I faithfully give a percentage of my income to our
church (10 percent, a tithe, is a classic, biblical standard).

Planned

What does God want me to do with God's stuff?
I plan on giving ahead in order to give
consistently to our church.

Occasional

What does God want me to do with my stuff?
I give to our church but not consistently.

First Time

What do I do with my stuff?
I have not given to our church.

Final Thoughts

Our biblical study shows that giving proves more profound than it might appear at first glance. When you illumine divine wisdom on giving, you see that—

- Giving expresses worship to God.
- Giving demonstrates spiritual maturity.
- Giving develops faith and exhibits trust.
- Giving invests in Christ's mission in the world.
- Giving frees us from consumerism.
- Giving flows from gratitude.
- Giving cares for others over ourselves.

People ignited on fire for Jesus Christ give generously. And when we generously give, we share in God's happiness, we bless others and we find joy, not only here on earth, but in eternity!

Acknowledgment

I thank God for my wife, Tamara, who sat beside me on our back porch as I typed away on the laptop. She graciously commented when I read sentences, and gave wise input, such as not to use too many words, which I've tried to do.

My editor, Iva Morelli, has once again been a joy as a writing partner. Her professional skills, and personal encouragement make the process more fun and the book better.

The Christ Fellowship Elders and Staff support me and enable me to write. Thank you. The family of Christ Fellowship first heard this teaching and encouraged me to share it. Thank you. It's a privilege and a joy to serve Jesus as your pastor.

All glory to God.

Recommended Resources

Randy Alcorn, *The Treasure Principle, Revised and Updated* (Colorado Springs: Multnomah, 2012).

Randy Alcorn, *Money, Possessions, and Eternity: A Comprehensive Guide to What the Bible Says about Financial Stewardship, Generosity, Materialism, Retirement, Financial Planning, Gambling, Debt, and More* (Carol Stream, IL: Tyndale, 2003).

Dave Ramsey, *The Total Money Make Over* (Nashville: Thomas Nelson, 2013).

Dave Ramsey, Financial Peace University, https://www.daveramsey.com/

Crown Ministries, https://www.crown.org/

Ron Blue, *Master Your Money: A Step-by-Step Plan for Experiencing Financial Contentment* (Chicago: Moody Press, 2016). https://ronblueinstitute.com/

Gene A. Getz, *Rich in Every Way: Everything God says about Money and Possessions* (New York: Howard Books, 2004).

John Cortines, Gregory Baume, *True Riches: What Jesus Really Said About Money and Your Heart* (Nashville: Thomas Nelson, 2019).

John Cortines, Gregory Baume, *God and Money: How We Discovered True Riches at Harvard Business School* (Peabody, MA: Rose Publishing, 2016). https://generousgiving.org/

About the Author

BRUCE B. MILLER

God has given Bruce the treasure of his wonderful wife, Tamara, and blessed them with five children, and now the gift of grandchildren. God used Bruce to plant Christ Fellowship in McKinney, Texas where he currently serves as senior pastor (CFhome.org). In his spare time, he loves spending time with Tamara, playing racquetball, hiking, using a chainsaw and sitting by an open fire with his chocolate Labrador, Calvin.

His passion for leadership development led to his first book, *The Leadership Baton*, written with Jeff Jones and Rowland Forman. Bruce's heart to see people live more joyful, fulfilled lives sparked the writing of *Your Life in Rhythm*, the forerunner to *Your Church in Rhythm* which applies the concepts of rhythmic living to local churches (BruceBMiller.com).

Bruce developed the innovative six-step WISDOM Process© which serves as a learning engine in the study guides for this book and others: *Big God in a Chaotic World—A Fresh Look at Daniel*; *When God Makes No Sense—A Fresh Look at Habakkuk*, and *Never the Same—A Fresh Look at the Sermon on the Mount*. Bruce provides wisdom for church leaders in his recent book, *Leading a Church in a Time of Sexual Questioning: Grace-Filled Wisdom for Day-to-Day Ministry*.

Bruce graduated Phi Beta Kappa from the University of Texas at Austin with a B.A. in Plan II, the Honors Liberal Arts Program; earned a master's degree in Theology from Dallas Theological Seminary; and did doctoral work at the University of Texas at Dallas in the History of Ideas. He taught theology for four years at Dallas Theological Seminary.

Bruce speaks and consults around the world. He founded the Centers for Church Based Training (http://ccbt.org). Bruce also founded and leads Dadlin ministries, an organization committed to helping people develop wisdom for life. Bruce's passion is to illumine wisdom that lights people on fire for Jesus Christ.

You can follow Bruce on:
Facebook
(https://www.facebook.com/BruceBMillerAuthor)

To invite Bruce to speak, contact him at:
Website (BruceBMiller.com)
where you can find all of his books

Other Resources

The publishing ministry of Dadlin ministries—an

organization committed to helping people develop wisdom for life.

Resources by Bruce B. Miller:

The Leadership Baton
Equips you with a solution to the need for quality leaders in local churches. Miller provides you with a biblical vision, a holistic approach and a comprehensive plan.

Your Life in Rhythm
Offers a realistic way to overcome our crazy, overly busy, stressed lives. Exposes the myth of living a "balanced" life. Miller presents "rhythmic living" as a new paradigm for relieving guilt and stress, so we can accomplish more of what matters most in life—with more freedom, peace, fulfillment and hope.

Your Church in Rhythm
Most pastors try to do everything at once, and they feel guilty if even one aspect of their church ministry is neglected in the process. Instead, Miller proposes replacing this exhausting notion of "balance" with the true-to-life concept of "rhythm." Churches, just like people, should focus on the seasons and the cycles of ministry programs. That way, leaders can avoid burnout by focusing only on each issue at the time that it matters most.

Big God in a Chaotic World—A Fresh Look at Daniel

Shows we can live faithfully in this sinful, out-of-control world when we get a fresh vision of our big God. Daniel opens our eyes to see the God who is bigger than the problems in our world, bigger than all our fears, fires and lions.

Same-Sex Marriage—A Bold Call to the Church in Response to the Supreme Court's Decision

In response to this cultural crisis, the church should step up with a Christ-like response that stuns the world, and draws people to Jesus Christ with counter-cultural love.

Same-Sex Wedding—Should I Attend?
Christians disagree on whether or not to attend a same-sex wedding. This book dives into the controversy, and helps us discover more options than simply to go or not to go.

When God Makes No Sense—A Fresh Look at Habakkuk
In this crazy world, it can seem like God is far off or indifferent. His failure to act makes no sense. Why do some people prosper and other people suffer? Miller helps us see that when life is shaking

you like a leaf in the storm, you can hold on to the unshakeable God who controls the storm.

Never the Same—A Fresh Look at the Sermon on the Mount
Jesus shocked and offended his original audience because he turned most people's view of life upside down. Follow Jesus' kingdom vision and you will stand out as a bright light in a dark world, stand up when storms come, and step up to receive God's eternal reward.

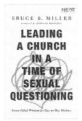

Leading a Church in a Time of Sexual Questioning: Grace-Filled Wisdom for Day-to-Day Ministry
In a time when sexual norms are changing rapidly, how can a local church be a place of grace—a loving community for all kinds of people—where everyone can flourish and disagreements are overcome in a Christ-like spirit while at the same time stay true to biblical standards?

For more information on current and upcoming books, go to BruceBMiller.com.

Dadlin Media
— wisdom for life —

McKinney, TX 75070

Notes

1. Rod Rogers, *Pastor Driven Stewardship* (Dallas: Brown Books Publishing, 2006), 71.

2. Randy Alcorn, *Money, Possessions and Eternity* (Wheaton, IL: Tyndale House, 1989), 234.

3. Gene A. Getz, *Real Prosperity* (Chicago: Moody Press, 1990), 124.

4. Getz, *Rich in Every Way* (West Monroe, LA: Howard Publishing, 2004), 314.

5. Randy Alcorn, *Money, Possessions and Eternity* (Wheaton, IL: Tyndale House, 1989), 268.

6. Scott Burns, *The Disciple of Giving*, "Asset Builder," December 25, 2005.

Made in the USA
Columbia, SC
25 January 2024